Fun Experiments

with

Forces and Motion

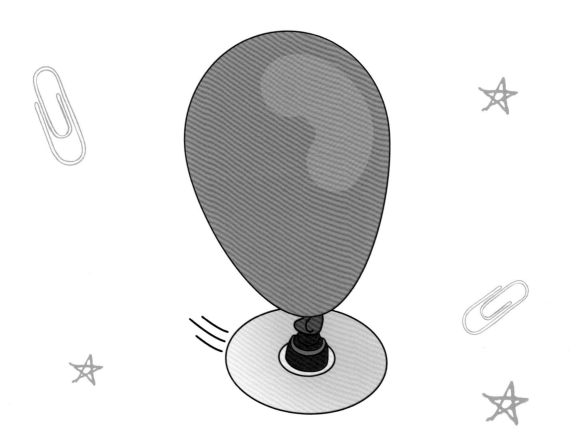

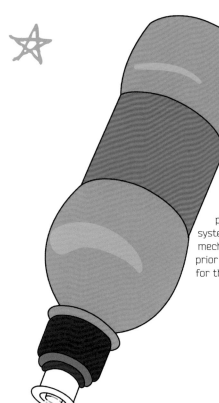

Thanks to the creative team:
Senior Editor: Alice Peebles
Fact checking: Tom Jackson
Design: www.collaborate.agency

Hungry Tomato®
A division of Lerner Publishing Group, Inc.
241 First Avenue North
Minneapolis, MN 55401 USA

For reading levels and more information, look up this title at www.lernerbooks.com.

Main body text set in Minya Nouvelle Regular 12/15.

Library of Congress Cataloging-in-Publication Data

The Cataloging-in-Publication Data for *Fun Experiments with Forces and Motion* is on file at the Library of Congress
ISBN 978-1-5124-3216-9 (lib. bdg.)
ISBN 978-1-5124-4997-6 (EB pdf)

Manufactured in the United States of America
1-41772-23533-4/14/2017

Fun Experiments

with

Forces and Motion

by Rob Ives
Illustrated by Eva Sassin

HUNGRY TOMATO®

Minneapolis

Safety First

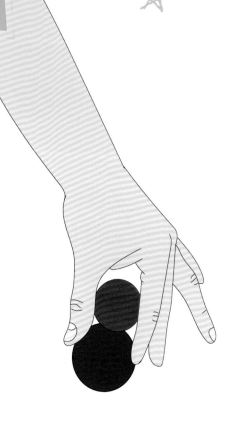

Take care and use good sense with these amazing science experiments—some are very simple, while others are trickier.

Each project includes a list of everything you will need. Most of the items are things you can find around the house, or they are things that are readily available and inexpensive to buy.

Be sure to check out the Amazing Science behind the projects and learn the scientific principles involved in each experiment.

Watch for this sign throughout the book. You may need help from an adult to complete these tasks.

Contents

Forces and Motion   6

Bottle Rocket   8

Ball into Orbit!   10

Balloon Hovercraft   12

Elastic-Band Dragster   14

Paper Plane   18

Candle Seesaw   22

Soap-Powered Boat   24

Warm-Air Spinner   26

Vortex   28

Glossary   30

Did You Know?   31

Index   32

Forces and Motion

Forces are at the heart of everything that happens. A force is basically a push or a pull. It makes things accelerate—that is, change speed or direction. Without forces, nothing would ever happen because all things have natural inertia. This means they stay stock still until they are forced into moving! Things fall because of the force of gravity. You pick up a drink using the force of your muscles.

Discover how to use forces to create motion and blast a rocket into the air, power a superfast dragster, lift a hovercraft, and much more. May the force be with you!

You Will need:

Bouncy balls in different sizes

Thumb tacks

Balloons

$\frac{7}{8}$-inch (25 mm) steel washers x2

Large and small paper clips

Long, thin household candle

Tea light

Ice pop craft sticks

Liquid soap

Aluminium drink cans

talcum powder

Talcum powder (baby powder)

Shallow tray

Thin craft foam sheet

Drink bottles with sports caps

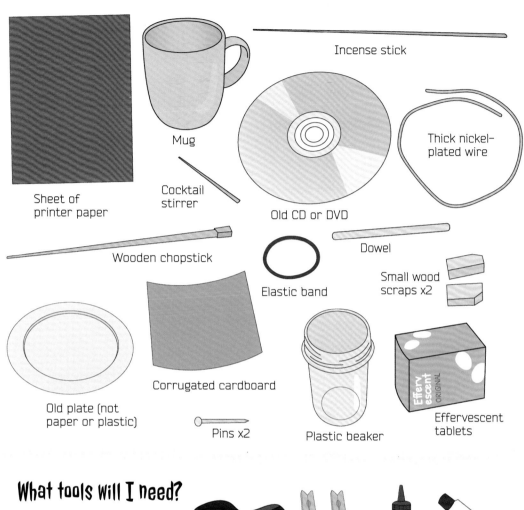

Sheet of printer paper

Mug

Cocktail stirrer

Incense stick

Old CD or DVD

Thick nickel-plated wire

Wooden chopstick

Elastic band

Dowel

Small wood scraps x2

Old plate (not paper or plastic)

Corrugated cardboard

Pins x2

Plastic beaker

Effervescent tablets

What tools will I need?

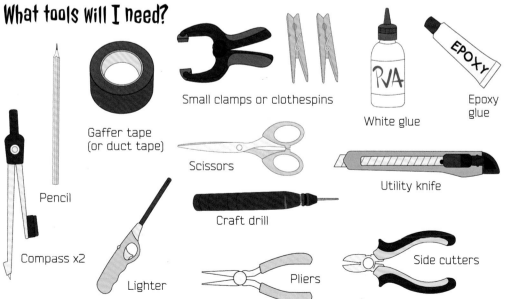

Pencil

Compass x2

Gaffer tape (or duct tape)

Lighter

Small clamps or clothespins

Scissors

Craft drill

White glue

Pliers

Epoxy glue

Utility knife

Side cutters

Bottle Rocket

A normal drink bottle turns into a mini rocket if it has enough propulsion. It may not land on the moon, but you'll be surprised at the whizzing power of fizz. So it's probably best to try this outside—in fact, DO try this outside!

You will need:

Drink bottle with sports cap

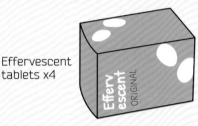

Effervescent tablets x4

Mug

1. Have four tablets ready to use.

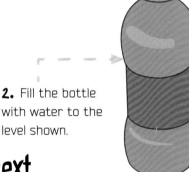

2. Fill the bottle with water to the level shown.

Complete these next steps as quickly as possible!

3. Break up the tablets and drop them in the water.

4. With the sports cap pressed down to close it, screw the lid on tight.

5. Shake the bottle a couple of times.

6. Place the bottle upside down in the mug.

7. **Step back!**

8. The pressure from the tablets builds up, and when it gets high enough, it blows the lid open, launching the rocket out of the mug and skywards!

Amazing Science

Rockets blast through space by burning fuel to make rapidly expanding gases. The push, or reaction, between the rocket and the gases drives the rocket forward. Here, the expanding gases from the effervescent tablets force the water out through the nozzle, giving lift-off.

Ball into Orbit!

Strange things happen when you bounce balls stacked together. Smaller does not necessarily mean weaker—it may mean the opposite! Find a suitable surface, such as a brick wall, so you can measure the height the balls reach when they bounce.

You Will need:

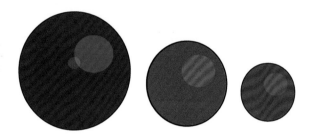

Superpower bouncy balls in different sizes

1. Drop a single ball and see what happens. You'll find it bounces lower than the height it's dropped from. If you bounce it on a hard surface, you can expect it to reach just under 70 percent of the height it's dropped from.

2. Things get interesting when you drop more than one ball together.

Start by holding two balls with the smaller one at the top. Let them drop straight down and watch what happens.

3. The first thing to notice is that the larger ball hardly bounces. It may bounce about 15 to 20 percent of the original bounce height.

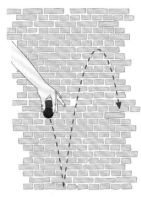

4. The smaller ball acts differently. It bounces much higher than the original drop—maybe even twice as high!

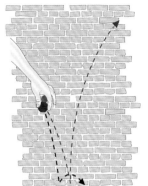

5. Try the same thing but with the very smallest ball at the top. Can you guess what will happen?

The smaller the ball, the higher it flies!

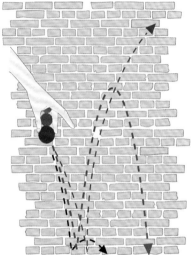

6. Now hold three balls with the smallest on top. Drop them straight so that they stay together as they fall.

Watch as the smallest ball goes into orbit!*
*almost

Amazing Science

Energy never disappears, but it can be transferred from one thing to another. Here you transfer the energy of a large ball bouncing to a smaller ball. It flies so high in the air, it's as if it was supercharged— which it is!

Balloon Hovercraft

Old CD or DVD

A hovercraft is a clever form of transport that moves along on a cushion of air, so it doesn't touch the surface below. This allows it to travel over ice and land as well as water.

Drink bottle with sports cap

Balloon

Tools you will need:
(see page 7)

✬ Epoxy glue

1. Use epoxy to glue the lid of the bottle over the hole in the CD.

2. Pull up the sports cap so that air can flow freely through it.

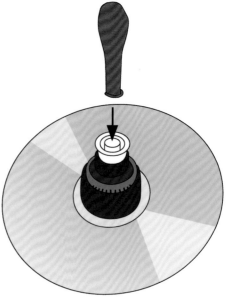

3. Fit the balloon over the lip of the sports cap.

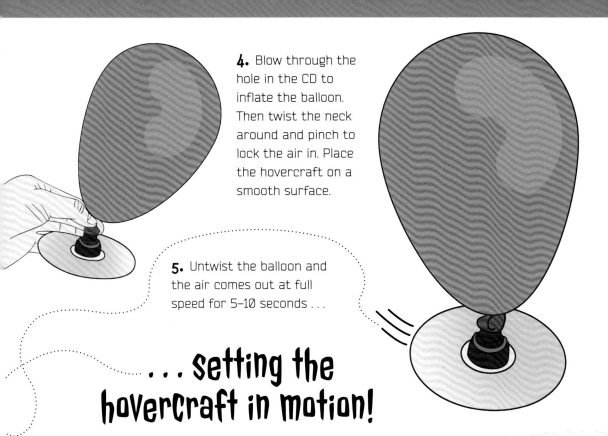

4. Blow through the hole in the CD to inflate the balloon. Then twist the neck around and pinch to lock the air in. Place the hovercraft on a smooth surface.

5. Untwist the balloon and the air comes out at full speed for 5–10 seconds . . .

. . . setting the hovercraft in motion!

Amazing Science

The air beneath a hovercraft is squeezed so that its push, or pressure, lifts the craft, letting it float over most surfaces. Here, the pressure of air outside squeezes the air inside the balloon and pushes it out under the disc, so the disc floats like a hovercraft.

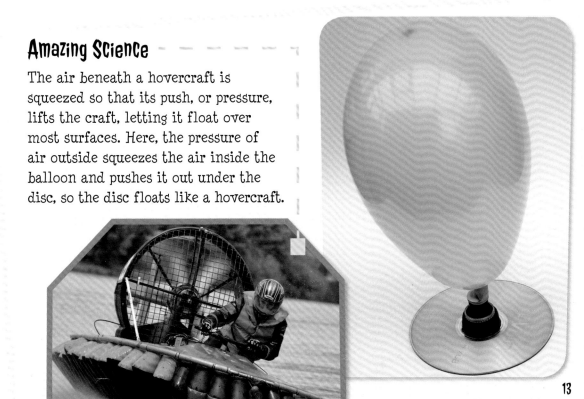

Elastic-Band Dragster

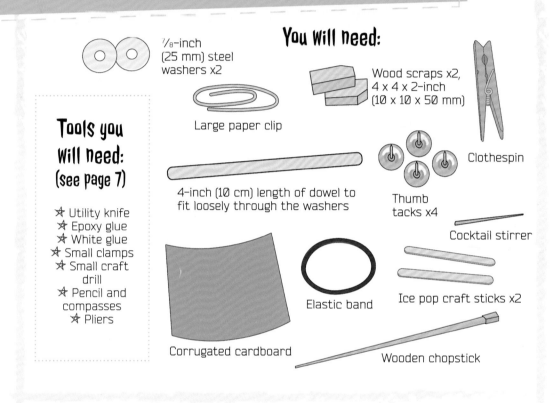

You will need:

⅞-inch (25 mm) steel washers x2

Large paper clip

Wood scraps x2, 4 x 4 x 2-inch (10 x 10 x 50 mm)

Clothespin

4-inch (10 cm) length of dowel to fit loosely through the washers

Thumb tacks x4

Cocktail stirrer

Corrugated cardboard

Elastic band

Ice pop craft sticks x2

Wooden chopstick

Tools you will need:
(see page 7)

✶ Utility knife
✶ Epoxy glue
✶ White glue
✶ Small clamps
✶ Small craft drill
✶ Pencil and compasses
✶ Pliers

Dragsters are cars that accelerate very rapidly. They burn rocket fuel to release its energy and provide the force to send the dragster whizzing away!

1. Use a utility knife to shave off a diagonal from one corner of each wood scrap. This will make room for the elastic band. Fix the wood pieces to the chopstick with epoxy glue and clamp them as it dries.

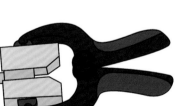

2. Use epoxy glue and thumb tacks to fix and pin the washers to the blocks, with the dowel threaded into place for the axle.

Thumb tack

3. Use a pencil and compasses and a utility knife to cut out four card circles: two 3-inch (2 x 80 mm), two 1.5-inch (2 x 40 mm). Make them into the two large back wheels as shown, using white glue.

3 in (80 mm)

1.5 in (40 mm)

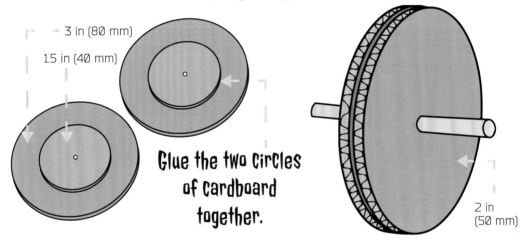

Glue the two circles of cardboard together.

2 in (50 mm)

4. Make the front wheel the same way with two 2-inch (50 mm) circles of card. Pierce a small hole in the center to fit the cocktail stick through as the axle.

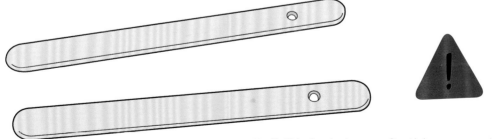

5. Drill holes in two craft sticks so that the front wheel axle is a loose fit.

6. Use pliers to help you unfold the paper clip and make a wire to coil fairly loosely around the end of the chopstick. Keep a hook at the end.

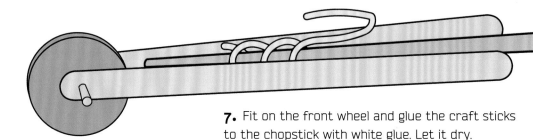

7. Fit on the front wheel and glue the craft sticks to the chopstick with white glue. Let it dry.

Cut open an elastic band and tie it to the wire hook.

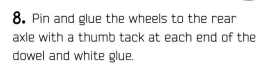

8. Pin and glue the wheels to the rear axle with a thumb tack at each end of the dowel and white glue.

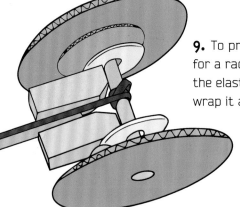

9. To prepare the car for a race, stretch out the elastic band and wrap it around the axle.

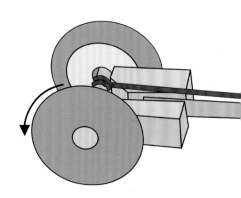

10. Turn the wheels backwards to stretch the elastic band and create the tension for it to race away.

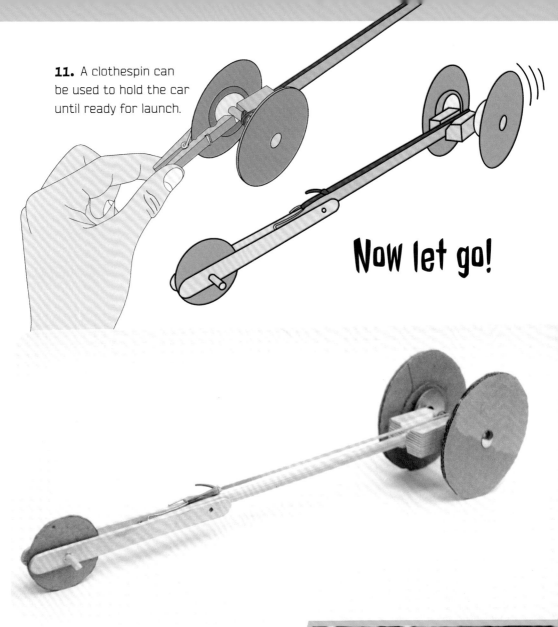

11. A clothespin can be used to hold the car until ready for launch.

Now let go!

Amazing Science

The more force you use, the faster things accelerate. Here, the force doesn't come from rocket fuel burning (of course!), but it is stored in the stretch of the elastic band. But the principle is the same.

Paper Plane

This paper aircraft is a fantastic little flyer. Just keep your lines straight and points and creases sharp!

You will need:

Single sheet of printer paper

Small paper clip

1. Fold the paper in half lengthwise, then open it up.

2. Fold it in half along the width. Keep this fold and fold along the previous crease, so it's folded into quarters.

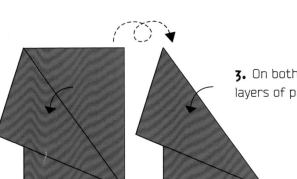

3. On both sides, fold back the two layers of paper along the diagonal.

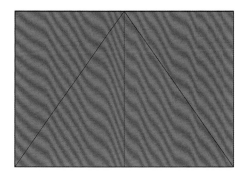

4. Open out the paper so that it is only half-folded.

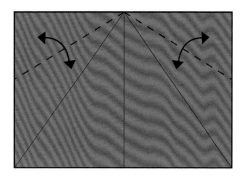

5. Fold in both layers from the center line as shown.

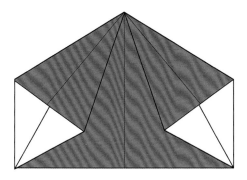

6. Open out and fold flat.

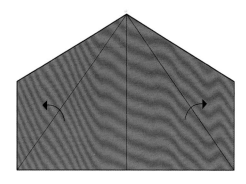

7. Fold the top layer of one side back along the diagonal. Fold in the top triangle over it. Match this on the lower layer. Repeat on the other side.

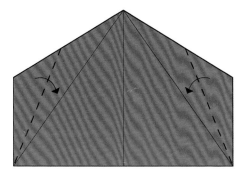

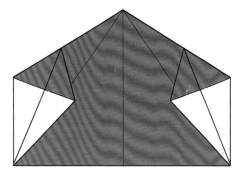

8. Fold out the top layer. Fold back the side edge as shown. Fold back the lower layer underneath.

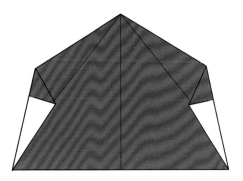

9. Repeat this process on the other side.

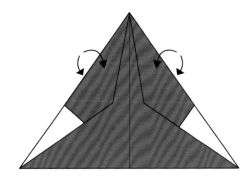

10. Fold the edges in, front and back.

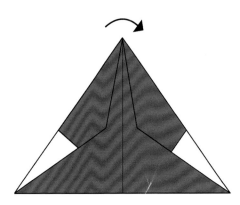

11. Fold the plane in half.

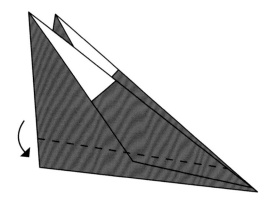

12. Fold the wings down by folding from the nose along the base of the wings.

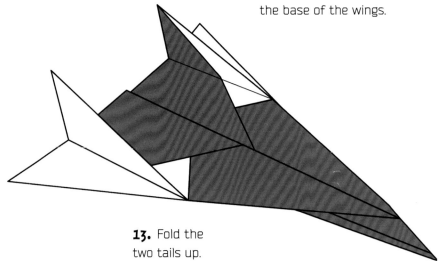

13. Fold the two tails up.

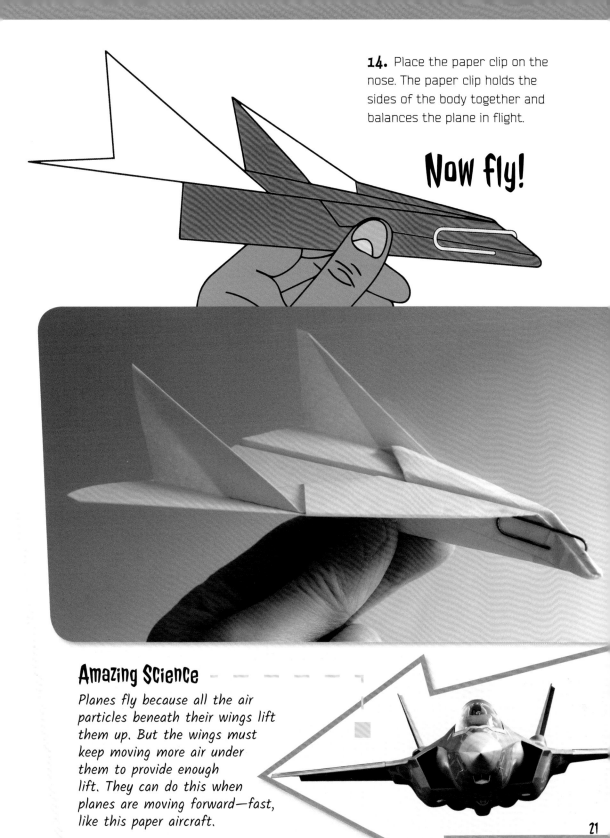

14. Place the paper clip on the nose. The paper clip holds the sides of the body together and balances the plane in flight.

Now fly!

Amazing Science

Planes fly because all the air particles beneath their wings lift them up. But the wings must keep moving more air under them to provide enough lift. They can do this when planes are moving forward—fast, like this paper aircraft.

Candle Seesaw

You Will need:

One long, thin household candle

Two pins

Old plate (not paper or plastic)

2 feet (60 cm) thick, nickel-plated wire

Shifting weight makes a candle rock back and forth . . .

Tools you Will need:
(see page 7)

✶ Pliers
✶ Side cutters
✶ Lighter

1. Trim the bottom off the candle, leaving the wick exposed. The candle now has a wick at each end.

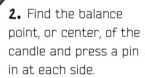

2. Find the balance point, or center, of the candle and press a pin in at each side.

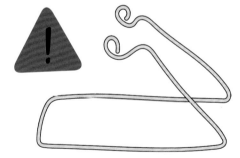

3. Make this balance frame from the wire. It should be slightly wider than the candle.

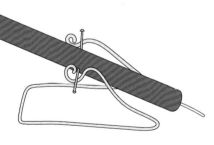

4. Drop the candle into position and place the seesaw on the old plate.

Do not place fingers, clothing, or any other materials near the flame. Extinguish the flame immediately upon completing the experiment.

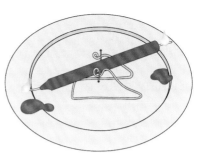

5. The candle will most likely be heavier on one side. Light it at the heavier end.

6. When the balance begins to change, light the other end of the candle.

7. As the candle burns, the lower end will burn faster, making that end lighter. The candle will then tilt up. The process will repeat over and over.

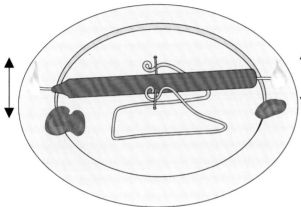

It's a moving seesaw!

Amazing Science

A seesaw stays level when the riders are balanced in weight. But if one leans forward, they go up because their weight has less leverage nearer the pivot. They lean back to go down again. The candle seesaws as either end becomes lighter as the wax melts and drips off the candle.

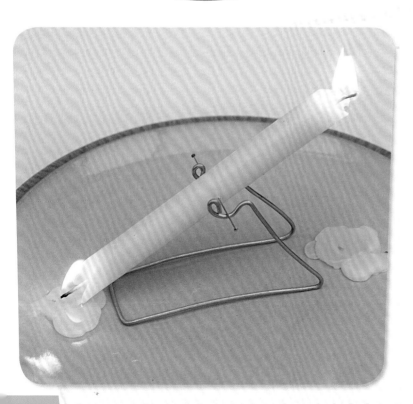

Soap-Powered Boat

This little boat is propelled forward when soap touches the water. Water has high surface tension, while soap has low surface tension. They have net force when they interact known as the Marangoni effect (see Amazing Science opposite).

Shallow tray

Liquid soap

talcum powder
Talcum powder (baby powder)

You will need:

Thin, close-celled craft foam, 4 x 3 in (10 x 7 cm)

Tools you will need:
(see page 7)

✷ Utility knife

1. To see the science at work, fill a shallow tray with water. Sprinkle a thin layer of talcum powder over the water.

2. Drop a single drop of liquid soap into the tray, A circle of clear water will quickly appear as the talcum powder is pushed back. The boat harnesses this amazing power.

3. Use a utility knife to cut the boat shape from the craft foam with a 1-inch (25 mm) hole and a slot at the back end.

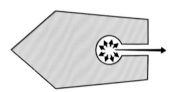

4. The boat has a circular hole in the body to take the drop of soap. The slot channels the soap out of the boat, powering it forward.

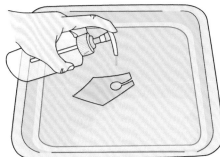

5. Float the boat on a new tray of water and drip a drop of soap into the hole in the boat.

The boat shoots forward!

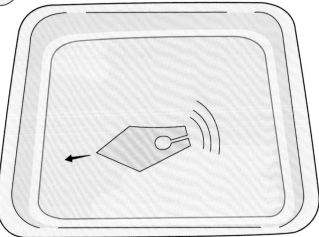

Amazing Science

Water molecules cling together at the surface, creating a skin held together by surface tension. A drop of soap breaks the high surface tension of the water so the boat moves. Small objects that are denser than water can also float due to surface tension.

Warm-Air Spinner

The spinner is powered simply by warm air rising from a candle flame.

Be careful with this activity as the edges of the can could be very sharp.

You will need:

Tea light

Aluminium drink can

Tools you will need:
(see page 7)

☆ Epoxy glue
☆ Kitchen scissors
☆ Small clamps or clothespins
☆ Lighter or matches

2 feet (60 cm) thick, nickel-plated wire

1. Cut the ends off the can with kitchen scissors.

2. Cut out this shape for the hub and fold it up. The sides of each triangle are 0.5 inches (15 mm).

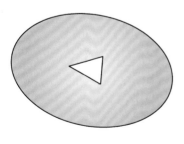

3. Cut out a 3.5-inch (90 mm) circle from the can and cut a hole that fits the hub in the center.

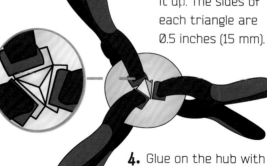

4. Glue on the hub with epoxy and secure with small clamps or clothespins until dry.

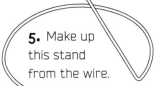

5. Make up this stand from the wire.

6. Cut and bend the circle into blades to make the propeller. One edge of each blade turns up, the other down.

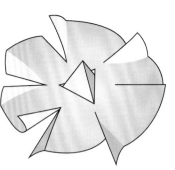

Do not place fingers, clothing, or any other materials near the flame. Extinguish the flame immediately upon completing the experiment.

7. Balance the propeller on the wire stand. Light a tea light under it.

Watch as the warm air makes it spin!

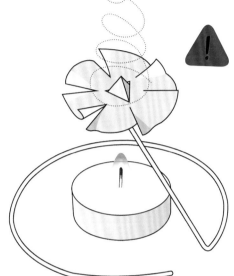

Amazing Science

The warm air rises and pushes against the underside of the spinner. The angle of the blades turns the vertical force of the rising air into a rotary movement.

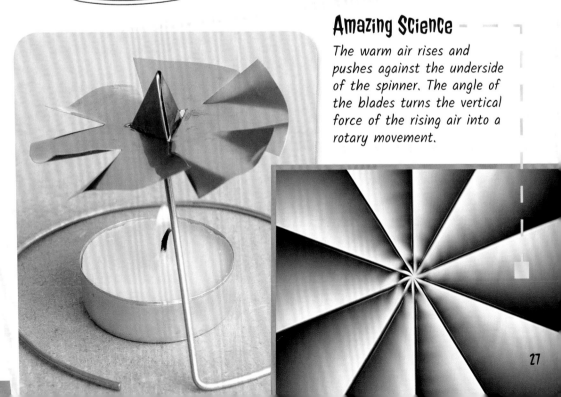

Vortex

A vortex is a rotating fluid or gas. It may form a spiral as it loses energy, but a smoke ring is a kind of vortex that is doughnut-shaped and rotates around itself.

You will need:

Incense stick

Balloon

Plastic beaker with a 3-inch (80 mm) neck

Tools you will need:
(see page 7)

✶ Scissors
✶ Gaffer tape (or duct tape)
✶ Lighter

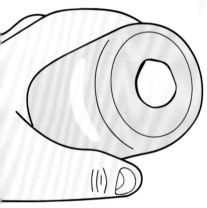

1. Cut a circular hole in the bottom of the plastic beaker.

2. Cut the top off a balloon.

3. Tie a knot in the stem of the balloon.

4. Stretch the balloon over the open end of the beaker.

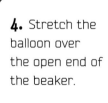

5. Tape the edges of the balloon to the beaker with gaffer tape (or duct tape).

6. Light a scented joss stick and fill the beaker with smoke. Make sure you don't touch the balloon with the joss stick as it will melt through quickly!

Do not place fingers, clothing, or any other materials near the flame. Extinguish the flame immediately upon completing the experiment.

7. Tap the balloon and a series of smoke rings will be created. The vortex moves slowly, but the air in each vortex spins fast. If you aim a vortex at a candle flame you will be able to blow it out!

Amazing Science

When air is compressed (squeezed), its particles are packed together. So, when the balloon is pushed inward, the smoke particles in the jar are punched together and make rotating smoke rings.

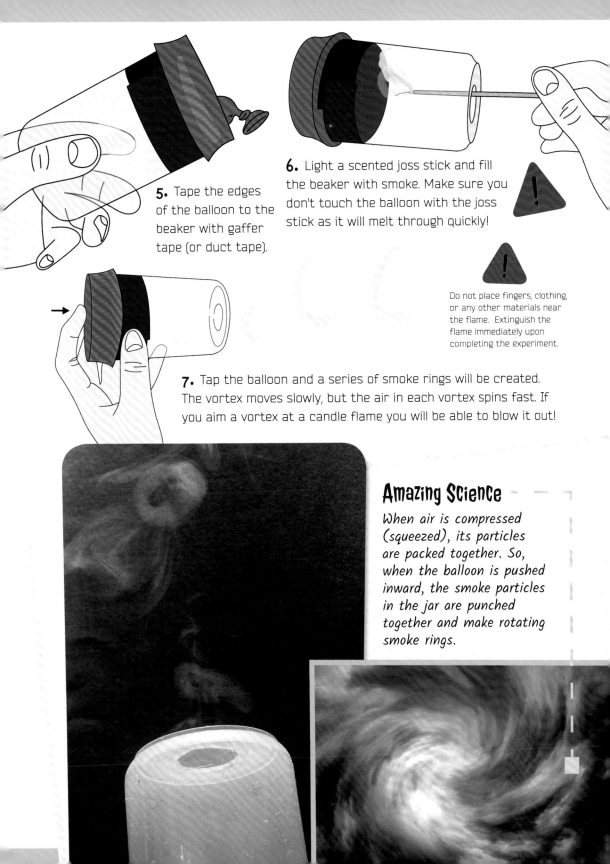

Glossary

air pressure: Air molecules are tiny and invisible, but together they can exert a considerable force on a surface. This force, or pressure, increases when extra air is added in a confined space or container, when pumping up a tire with air, for example.

hovercraft: A vehicle that can travel just above the surface of land or water by floating on a cushion of air that also provides propulsion

pivot: The midpoint of an object or lever system. It is the turning point around which the lever moves. If extra force or weight is applied at one end, the object or lever will move at the other end.

rocket: A missile or spacecraft that gets its thrust (pushed forward) from a rocket engine. The rocket carries its own oxygen to burn its fuel. As the fuel burns, it produces a stream of gases to propel the rocket forwards. Launch rockets are several rockets linked together. As each rocket uses up its fuel, it breaks away, making the rest of the unit lighter and faster.

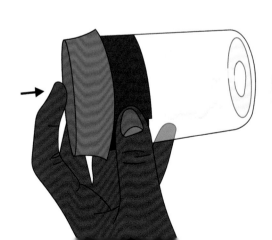

Did You Know?

★ Robert Goddard built the first rocket in 1926. It climbed 40 ft (12 m) in 2.5 seconds.

★ British inventor Christopher Cockerell had a battle to get his hovercraft design taken seriously. The Navy called it a plane not a boat, the Air Force called it a boat not a plane. It made a successful test-crossing of the English Channel in 1959, then really took off in the 1960s.

In 1995, American Bob Windt set a record 85.38 mph (137.4 km/h), racing his hovercraft on Portugal's River Douro.

★ A rocket has to travel at about 20 times the speed of sound to reach space from Earth. That's 4.9 mps (7.9 km/s). Many have done so, including the United State's Atlas V, to put satellites in orbit. On March 1, 2017, it accomplished its 70th mission.

| US Saturn V | Soviet N1 | US Titan IV | US Atlas V | US Space Shuttle | India PSLV | Japan H-II A | China, Long March 3B |

Not to scale.

INDEX

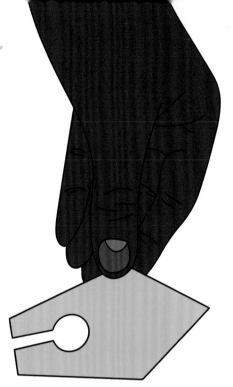

air pressure, 13, 30

balloon hovercraft, 12–13
bottle rocket, 8–9
bouncing balls, 10–11

candle seesaw, 22–23

dragster, elastic-band, 14–17

flight, 21
forces and motion, 6

hovercraft, 12–13, 30–31

paper airplane, 18–21

pivot, 30

rocket power, 9, 14, 30–31

seesaw effect, 22–23
smoke rings, 28–29
soap-powered boat, 24–25
surface tension, 25

tools, 6–7
transfer of energy, 11

vortex, 28–29

warm-air spinner, 26–27

The Author

Rob Ives is a former math and science teacher, now a designer and paper engineer living in Cumbria, UK. He creates science- and project-based children's books, including *Paper Models that Rock!* and *Paper Automata*. He specializes in character-based paper animations and all kinds of fun and fascinating science projects, and he often visits schools to talk about design technology and demonstrate his models.

The Illustrator

Eva Sassin is a freelance illustrator born in London, UK. She has always loved illustrating, whether it be scary, fun monsters or cute, sparkly fairies. She carries a sketchbook everywhere, but she has even drawn on the back of receipts if she's forgotten it! In her free time, she travels around London to visit exhibitions and small cafés where she enjoys sketching up new ideas and characters. She is also a massive film buff!

Picture Credits (abbreviations: t = top; b = bottom; c = center; l = left; r = right)
© www.shutterstock.com:

9 br, 13 bl, 17 br, 21 br, 25 br, 27 br, 29 br, 31 tr.

Alamy credit - 31 cl.